To. _____

From. _____

A Tale of Two College Graduates

Who Landed the Interview

Jeff and Amy

Jim Serger

A Tale of Two College Graduates

Who Landed the Interview

Amy And Jeff

Jim Serger

A Tale of Two College Graduates Who Landed the Interview
Amy and Jeff

Published by: Red Bike Publishing

Published in the United States of America
www.redbikepublishing.com

Library of Congress Control Number: 2022933964

ISBN 13: 978-1-936800-39-1

DEDICATION

This book is dedicated to all college graduates—give them a reason to hire you.

Amy's Tale

It had been over a week since Amy had her first interview with FarmPond. As she exited the interview, Frank, from FarmPond Human Resources who conducted the interview, told her it would be about ten days or so until she heard back regarding whether she would be moving forward to a second interview with Mary, the Vice President.

Like every day, Amy started with a 6:30 a.m. alarm, by 6:45 Amy had her coffee brewing and had taken her dog for a morning walk. By 7:00 Amy was reading the highlights of the day's news and checking up on her emails and social media—making sure she was in the know.

Amy was a morning person, always ready to tackle the day's obstacles. She would adapt and conquer her daily routine, as well as adjust on the fly and navigate back on course, if need be, to complete the day in a positive, upbeat way.

Amy paced around her off-campus apartment at State University, a few cars zipped by the closed windows, a few dogs were barking off in the distance, and the brakes of the local city bus could be heard stopping to pick up passengers at the corner.

Amy knew the window of being called back was shrinking, however Amy, the hard-nosed young lady that she was, knew she gave it her best in the two-hour interview with Frank from HR. This being Monday morning, coming out of the weekend Amy's attitude was on point, and she knew by Wednesday or Thursday she would hear something.

By 8:00, Amy fed her dog Hank, ate her normal go to meal of oatmeal and a banana, got her workout clothes on, and leashed Hank for their usual morning one-mile walk. Once back at the apartment, Hank jumped up on the couch and settled down for his morning nap. Amy proceeded to turn on her morning workout routine to get the blood pumping. After 45 minutes Amy stopped, drenched in sweat, and began her cool down, when her phone rang.

Sue, her great college friend, called to see how she was and to check if FarmPond had called her back. Amy said, "No." Sue understood it was only day eight. Sue asked if she wanted to have dinner on Thursday night after work. Amy replied, "Yes, of course I do." So, their normal mid-week get together was lined up at the local pizza dive on Short Vine Street right by campus. "Love you Amy," Sue said. "Love you too," Amy replied, and she said, "I'll text you later. I have to be at work in about an hour."

Four years ago, at freshman orientation, Amy learned about the various jobs available on campus. Amy, being athletic and outgoing, was in the Student Fitness Center on the campus tour when the guide stated that college students could work a few hours a week at various campus spots—the cafeteria, the library, the bookstore, the student union, and the on-campus fitness building.

Amy was showered and ready to go to her job—the same job she had off and on in college, depending on the semester. Amy was able to walk there from her apartment, just a little over half a mile, but living on campus her freshman and sophomore year it was just a hop, skip and a jump. Walking to work Amy usually ran into a few fellow students. Today, Jerry yelled from the other side of the street, "Did you get the job?" Amy replied, "I haven't heard back." With that, Jerry's buddy yelled over, "You've got this Amy, hang in there." Amy with a big smile, and blushing yelled over, "Thanks guys, see you over the weekend."

By 10:45 Amy was in the building all set and ready for her 7-hour shift—which included lifeguarding from 11:00-1:00, weight room monitoring student IDs from 1:00-3:00, a little 30-minute break for lunch, and from 3:30 till 6:00 Amy was in charge of student photos, data entry, and answered the campus fitness room's phone. Amy loved it, the friends she made because of landing this job were unbelievable, and she was very aware that she only had two weeks left.

She graduated just three weeks back, May 15th to be exact. Amy loved college life, but her four years at State were ending soon—for Amy to stay on at the campus Fitness Center she would have to enroll in fall classes and work on her Master's Degree. However, Amy knew she needed to hit the work force, and work on her Master's in the future after she had a few years of real-life experience under her belt. FarmPond was just the company to gain that experience. She was ready for the call.

Per usual, Amy left the Center around 6:30 p.m. Her colleagues and she would joke, have a few laughs, and talk about the day before she would walk back home. On the way home, Amy usually ran into her former freshman Business 101 Professor, Professor Jones. They would stop, and talk for five minutes or so, and he would remind her, just as he did freshman year, "There is only one of you, be the best you."

Amy loved that quote by Professor Jones. She loved it so much that for her college graduation present her parents, who had heard it so many times over the last four years, gave her a wooden plaque with those words carved into it. It hangs on the wall to the right of her front door. As she heads out, those words "There is only one of you, be the best you" are what she carries with her and strives to live by each day.

Amy made it home quick, fed Hank, and cooked up her evening meal, or the normal go to meal when nothing was planned, ramen noodles. She sat in her cozy recliner, which she had purchased at the local thrift shop a few years back, and ate her dinner. She watched a little television, no cable but just local channels—Amy wanted to save money, plus she wasn't that into television. Amy was more into reading, so as her meal settled, Amy dove into her current book, which was her book group's latest choice. Amy had been in a book club since back in the dorms her freshman year. Her whole floor was in on it. Every two weeks they got together to talk, laugh, and bounce ideas off each other. Friendships blossomed and grew. Only now it was down to just eight girls—eight close friends, who got along so well. Eight friends that Amy knew would be life-long friends.

By the end of the evening, Amy had texted or received phone calls from numerous people, including Mom and Dad, who wanted to know about FarmPond. Mom was so worried, asking question after question and Dad was so excited too, giving her his dad speech, which was just a ring-side manager pep talk. She loved them both so much.

By 11:00 p.m. Amy was off to bed, hoping that tomorrow would be the big day. At 6:30 a.m. the alarm went off, and Amy was up and at it. Hank was out, morning meal down the hatch, and 45-minute workout complete, this time it was yoga. On cue, she received her normal call from Sue about FarmPond and confirmed their dinner for

Thursday. Amy loved Sue. "Of course, YES Sue, I will be there, and I hope to share with you some good news." Sue stated, "Amy, if they don't hire you, they are idiots." Amy responded upbeat, "Thanks Sue, I hear you, I gave my best interview, so I just know they will call me back, I just know it." Sue, who was feeling very protective, said, "If they don't, I'll go down there myself and tell them what's what. I've been taking Krav Maga and I'm not afraid to use it!" Amy started laughing and soon Sue was laughing, too. Laughter was a big part of their friendship. So many great times and the best of friends, always having each other's back. Amy said, "Yes Sue, you'll show them who's boss." With that, Amy said, "Goodbye, Sue." "Goodbye, Amy, make it a great day." Amy got ready for work and took Hank for one more short walk, and at 10:30 was out the door. She touched the sign with her right hand saying to herself, "There is only one of you, be the best you."

Today was a different day for Amy at the campus fitness center—she was the tour guide from 11:00-1:00 for potential students. She loved this day, for one day a week she could share her passion and school spirit for State with students who might attend in the fall. She loved to lead a group, loved to answer questions—for her knowledge of the school was on display, and the visitors felt it. From 1:00-3:00, Amy worked the phones, and from 3:00-6:00 Amy was the facility safety officer, making her rounds so students understood how to use the equipment correctly and safely. She also made sure the facility grounds were orderly and neat. She always said cheerfully, "If you need help, please just ask. My name is Amy."

At 6:30 p.m., after conversing with her fellow staffers and students, she was out the door and once again, as it always happened, she ran into Professor Jones. Today Professor Jones threw something her way, which she had heard a million times, "Are you being the best you today?" "Yes, Professor Jones, I am the best me today." "Very good, keep it up. It is supposed to rain tomorrow, more reason to be the best you." "Yes, Sir," stated Amy. As Professor Jones crossed the street he called back, "Have a super evening, Amy." "You too, Professor Jones."

"Why did he tell me it was going to rain," Amy wondered aloud, but that was Professor Jones, no matter how bad things might get, be the best you. She smiled and sprinted all the way home. New record, 6 minutes in an all-out sprint. Her best time was 6:45—she knocked off 45 seconds, must have been Professor Jones' pep talk, or that all the lights had the walk sign, she laughed. As she approached her front door, her phone rang, it was a number that was not familiar. Her heart raced.

Amy answered the phone right away, "Hello." "Your car warranty is about to expire," said the computer-generated voice. With that, Amy hung up and a slight smirk and laugh came over her, just then her neighbor popped into the hallway and said, "Hi Amy." She said, "Yes, hello there Mrs. Frand." Mrs. Frand had lived in the apartment complex forever, a retired State Professor, who loved State so much, that she consistently gave her time volunteering at the State hospital for children. She read to the kids three times a week for a few hours. They adored her. She had been a terrific neighbor to Amy, and Amy, being good hearted, had watched over her, too. She checked on her when the weather was bad and had taken her to the store a few times, and to campus activities. Mrs. Frand was kind of a mom away from home. "Have you heard anything from that company you interviewed with?" "No, not yet," said Amy— "Good things come to good people and you're good people," Mrs. Frand said graciously and with a warm tone. "Thank you, Mrs. Frand. If you need anything let me know and have a great night." "You too, Amy," Mrs. Frand said, and "Thank you, for all you do for me." Amy said, "You're welcome, off to grab Hank." "Yes Hank, go, go, go I'll talk with you later," Mrs. Frand said and pointed to the door... "Go, Go, Go."

Amy grabbed Hank and headed down to the Bark Park—routine in check, then back to the apartment—texting and talking with her parents along the way. Nothing new to share with them, however her parents showered her with support, and told her that Grandma and Grandpa were so proud of her, too. Her sister even texted to tell her to keep the eye on the prize, normal sister quick text. She was busy at her own college; she was a sophomore, having fun and keeping her grades up with all her activities. Big sister influence was working.

Amy nodded off to sleep, eyes closed, eyes open, eyes closed, eyes open all night, could be the humidity, it was high, grey clouds were rolling in and the scent of rain was in the air. "Professor Jones was right—it is going to rain," Amy thought. With that, her eyes closed, and stayed closed.

Amy tossed and turned all night long—she glanced at the clock, 1:00 a.m., 4:00 a.m., and finally at 6:30 a.m. her alarm went off. Even Hank, all night long was on the bed and off the bed, on the bed, off the bed. A small tapping at her window could be heard—now she understood why she didn't sleep well—it had started to rain, just like Professor Jones said it would—even a little rumble in the distance could be heard. Hank was startled a few times, but the morning came with just a few sprinkles—the heavy stuff must have come and gone in the middle of the night.

Amy hooked up Hank—quick out and to the point, he hated the rain. Back in, fed him, and she started her oatmeal and banana routine. Today Amy's schedule at work was a half-day, she was only in from 11:00-3:00. "Can't get these kids into overtime," she laughed to herself knowing that big things were on the horizon. Workout, "Check!" She yelled out when done, took a quick shower, and headed off to campus.

As she opened the door, she touched the sign on the way out and said, "Today is the day I will hear back from them." She popped open her umbrella and took off, with a quick pace to campus. A little drizzle and a few puddles, which she zig-zagged around like a barracuda— quick and fast—as she approached the center, she could see the sun trying to peek through, as if a sign to her that things were about to happen.

Arriving fifteen minutes early, as she always did, Amy grabbed her clipboard and was off to the front desk. Today, since it was a short day, she would just check IDs for two hours and lifeguard her last two. As she maintained her station, her boss Ann asked if she had heard anything from the Farm, yet. Amy stated, she had not. Ann, in a mentor voice, said, "Amy, if you need anything at all please ask me and I'll do my best to help you." "I really appreciate that, Ann," Amy replied, knowing that Ann was a State athlete and had worked with the school since graduating a few years back. Amy knew Ann always rooted for her—just had to be the boss first and a leader and mentor second. "ID please," Amy said as her first patron came in, "Okay, thanks have a super workout." As she always said after confirming they were affiliated with the school.

About 35 minutes into her routine, her phone rang, and it was a phone number that she did recognize. "Hello, this is Amy."— "Amy, this is Frank from FarmPond, how are you today?" With that, Amy smiled from ear to ear and hit the help button which was a direct line for Ann to come to her assistance. "Hi Sir, I am well—I have been looking forward to this phone call." "Great Amy, and I am so happy to call you, as well. We would love for you to come in for a final interview, which will be with our Vice President, Mary Phillips. Does Monday at 1:00 p.m. work for you?" "Yes, Sir," Amy said with a crackle of excitement in her voice. "Monday at 1:00 p.m. is perfect. I really appreciate the opportunity Frank, it means the world to me." "Amy, we look forward to seeing you. Park in the garage like you did before, take the stairs to the lobby, then, take the elevator to the 6th floor—not 5th for me, but 6th for Mary Phillips. The receptionist will greet you, and she will take you in for the interview." "Yes Frank, that sounds good. I look forward to Monday," Amy said, with a smile so big that everyone in the fitness center could see her gleaming with joy. "Okay Amy, we will see you at 1:00 p.m. on Monday, have a terrific weekend," Frank said, with a hint of joy in his voice. "Thank you, Sir, I will—you as well, and thank you for calling. You've made my week." "Good-bye Amy." "Good-bye Frank."

Ann, who had taken over Amy's station while she was on the phone, also had a huge smile and jumped up out of her seat, seeing how Amy's eyes were glazed over, she was red in the face, and had a slight stare of amazement. Ann knew Amy had received the call. Amy, jumping up and down now, was screaming, "They called me back! They called me back!" Ann gave her the biggest hug, a hug of pure comfort for she knew Amy deserved this second interview. Amy calmed down, but still radiated pure glee. She resumed her station and waited till 3:00 p.m. to tell anyone—that's the respect Amy had for her employers, and why FarmPond called her back. She was committed.

At three on the dot, she sprinted all the way home—jumping over puddles, curbs, and even jaywalking to get home. New record, 5:45—15 seconds faster than the day before. The sun was shining. She unlocked the door and gave Hank the biggest hug, and they danced a little in the kitchen. She took him out and back in, fed him, and proceeded to call Sue to tell her all about it.

Sue said, "We still on for pizza tomorrow night?" "Of course, yes we are," Amy said at the top of her lungs. And at the same time the girls yelled "Yippie!" Amy said, "What do I wear for the interview? Heels, flats, a dress, pants. Hair up or hair down. A purse or no purse—red dress or navy." "Slow down Amy, slow down. We will go over all of it over pizza," Sue said in a reassuring voice. "See you then Sue, 6 o'clock, I love you." Click....

Thursdays Amy does not have to work—for that is her laundry day, grocery day, ironing day, get things done day and most important, spend time one-on-one with Hank day. She normally took him down to the tiny river that runs around downtown. He dipped into the water, they played fetch, and he got to carry around sticks in his mouth. Big day for Hank and Amy—they usually even got an ice-cream for the ride home. So, she said right to Hank's face, "We are keeping our special day tomorrow."

That night after 6:00 p.m., she called her mom and dad—respecting that her dad was a high school principal, and her mom was a nurse—she knew they couldn't talk at three—school letting out and change of shift at the hospital—so six was a good time to call and share the great news. She told them all about it, "Monday at 1:00 p.m., downtown." Her mom and dad repeated themselves over and over like a broken record, "We love you, and we are so proud of you." Just like they have always done her whole life. Dad gave a little more advice than normal, like most dads do—knowing that Mom was just so nervous and excited. Dad playing the cool and calm role—explained to Amy, that FarmPond didn't just call anyone back, they called her. "You are awesome and will bring so much passion to FarmPond." Amy said, "Thanks," and believed her dad was right. Dad and Mom simultaneously said, "We love you, Amy." "I love you both too and thanks for always supporting me."

Amy knew Thursday was going to be a great day—sleep in a little if she could. A Hank doggy road trip, dinner with Sue, a good workout, read for sure, and most of all, plan her attack, and attack her plan for the interview.

On Friday, same routine as normal for a workday, 11:00-6:00, then right home, she thought to herself. But it's Thursday, her day to get things done, then dinner with Sue. Sue has been her sidekick and friend since day one four years ago in the dorm. That night Sue and she went over her resume, highlighting the strengths that Amy had to offer, and weaknesses that she could work toward adjusting. Amy loved to talk, so Sue reminded her to focus on Mary's questions, listen, then respond. No guessing on what Mary had to say, listen thoughtfully, and respond, really pay attention, different than the kind listening she did with her friends. Amy understood and they practiced over a few slices of pizza. Sue even tossed a couple questions her way. Amy responded well, then they laughed and laughed. Knowing that Amy was as ready as ever.

Friday came and went fast. Friday night, she laid out her wardrobe for the interview, and once again went over her past accomplishments. Saturday, she worked a half-day, 11:00-3:00, and met up with Sue, Jerry, and Tommy as well as others at Tommy's house for a small party, as they normally did over the weekend. The house rotated each weekend. Everyone was so excited for Amy. Jerry, who Amy dated off and on part of her freshman and sophomore years, was Amy's best guy friend, and he was so happy for her—saying over and over that she deserved the very best, and FarmPond was going to get the best. Tommy and she met after he transferred over from another college. They were in the engineering department together and worked in the lab together on and off. Everyone gave her hugs, gave her congratulations, but Amy said, "The verdict is still out. Monday at one o'clock will be the deciding factor."

Sundays Amy normally didn't have to work, however her boss, Ann, was able to switch Amy's schedule to allow her off on Monday for the interview. Amy hated to work Sundays, but this Sunday she was happy to be there. It was only a half-day, so she knew it would fly by. She just needed to do her work, keep her normal work routine, and she'd be home soon. Sue was coming over at 4:00 p.m., it was a girls' evening. Spaghetti dinner, watch a corny movie, put Amy at ease, and take the edge off—it worked. Sue looked over Amy's outfit of choice,

"Perfect," she said. "You're going to look great and be great," Sue stated with a rush of excitement. They mapped out how far of a drive it was—35 minutes, so they agreed that she should leave 1 hour early—12 noon, allowing 25 minutes for red lights, traffic, or whatever may be out of the norm. Arrive in the garage, go over a few things, then walk up and be in the lobby at 12:50.

Monday 6:30 alarm was beeping, Amy leashed up Hank—morning stroll was complete, fed Hank, morning oatmeal complete, morning cup of joe done. She put on her workout clothes and took Hank for a 1-mile walk—burn off some energy. Back at the apartment, Amy looked over her wardrobe again. "Perfect!" Amy was still a bit hyper with excitement. She looked in the mirror above her dresser—"Hi, I am Amy, very nice to meet you ma'am." "Hi, I am Amy, great to see you ma'am."— "Hi, I am Amy, good afternoon, ma'am, thanks for seeing me."

It was only 9:30 and Amy's brain was starting to run—so she said, "I need a 45-minute workout, exercise is good for the brain coach always said." With that, Amy was at ease, her go-to-routine never fails. At 10:30, she took Hank on one last quick stroll and got ready to go. 11:30, Amy had showered, and was dressed for success, hair and make-up done, and with one last look in the mirror—her phone rang, it was Mom. "Amy, I just wanted to say how much I love you, be yourself and enjoy this moment, you deserve it." "Thanks Mom, I love you too, —I'll call you the moment it's over." "Okay dear—just be you." "Yes, Mom—got to go, I love you."

With two minutes to spare, Amy gave Hank a kiss, and was in the car at high noon—right on time and headed out for FarmPond.

Amy hit every single red light, however because she left early, she arrived in the parking garage at 12:40. She looked herself over in the mirror one more time, and with one last lint brush roll she grabbed her purse and walked up to the lobby—hit the elevator button, stepped in, and spun around with a smile from ear to ear. She hit the 6th floor button—the door closed, one big deep breath and the door opened, with a nod of confidence she stepped out and proceeded to the receptionist desk. "Hello, I am Amy. I have a 1 o'clock appointment with Mary Phillips."— "Yes Amy, please have a seat and Mary will be right with you."— "Yes ma'am, thank you," Amy replied with a rush of excitement over her.

Amy took a seat on the leather chair overlooking the city— "What a view," she said to herself. "Nice to meet you." "Hello." "Thank you." "Yes." "Handshake."—all racing through Amy's thoughts— another big deep breath was needed to calm her down, then she said to herself—"Amy, be the best YOU." "Amy," the receptionist said. "Yes," Amy said. "Mary will see you now." With that, Amy stood up, smile on, purse straps over her left shoulder, and the receptionist opened the huge mahogany wood doors with solid brass handles, and there right in front of her about fifteen feet away was Mary standing up behind her glass desk, with books, awards, and certificates displayed on her back shelves.

Mary stepped out from around her desk and met Amy halfway— with her right hand the two shook hands, "Amy, it is so nice to finally meet you. I am Mary. I have read over all of your accomplishments, and Frank has told me wonderful things about you." "Yes Mary, very nice to meet you as well, what an amazing office you have and what a terrific view of the city," Amy stated, with a Christmas card worthy smile. A calmness came over Amy, after hearing Mary's words.

Mary and Amy proceeded to sit down in two leather chairs with a small glass table between them. There on the table was Amy's resume, as well as two coffee cups and a small pot. "Would you like some coffee?" Mary asked, "Or would you like a glass of water?" "Yes, coffee is fine, thank you," Amy said. Then a small conversation commenced, and after two minutes of friendly chit chat, Mary asked Amy a starter question, that Amy didn't see coming. "Have you ever read the play Macbeth?"—Amy responded right away, "Why, yes I have. I think the play is incredible, love the drama. Shakespeare has a way of making his villains so relatable, even though they do horrible things. Oh, and the fortune telling witches." "I really remember the three witches," Mary interjected. "Double double, toil and trouble/parties burn and nonsense bubble. Is that how it goes?" Mary asked. Amy smiling said, "Why yes, something like that." "And I like King Duncan. He seems like a generous King," Mary said with excitement. "Yes, I really like Shakespeare," Amy said with a bit of passion. "Yes," Mary agreed with a smile on her face.

Suddenly, Amy was at ease, very relaxed, as if she was at a book group with friends. She thought, I guess that was the trick question—"Yes, I nailed it," Amy thought to herself. Mary, with a sip of her coffee, hunkered down, and dove right into the interview.

"I see you were on the swim team," Mary stated. "Yes ma'am, my freshman, sophomore and junior year," Amy said with confidence. "But I had to pull out due to a shoulder injury I suffered riding horses. I was thrown from a horse while vacationing with my parents, I landed and tore my rotator cuff. Thanks to rehab my shoulder is fine, but I had to give up swimming. The 1 mile was just too much; however, I was able to stay on as a manager of the team for my senior year. It stung not to swim, but I still had my teammates and finished out my final season as part of the team, continuing to offer my services anyway I could. Additionally, I still was able to keep my co-captain status."

"Very good, Amy! Team—that's what our business is about," Mary said with gusto. "Yes, Mary I love team—like coach said, Together Everyone Achieves More," Amy shared with zest. "Yes Amy, no individualism here—we are all a team,"—Mary replied, showing Amy she is a part of the team as well, not just a leader.

"Amy, I'd like to hear about South America," Mary asked inquisitively. "Yes ma'am. At the end of my freshman year I wanted to find an internship, but due to my freshman status no one would take me on, so I contacted my church and they were able to set me up with a local charity that builds homes for the poor in South America. My pastor helped me because I had been involved in building homeless shelters with my family and friends since 4th grade. I was offered the opportunity, and the State college fitness center was able to give me three weeks off to go down and volunteer. It was such a wonderful experience." Amy was so proud of the kinship she developed down there.

"Your State college fitness center, what is that?" asked Mary with a hint of wonder. "When I was a freshman, I wanted to be more involved with the college. Not just swim but, work on campus. I was living in the dorms, at the time, and I wanted to make more friends and have a little spending money, too. I applied for the open position, and campus gave me a floating schedule, so I was able to work 10 to 30 hours a week, when not swimming."

"Oh, that's great Amy—did your grades keep up?" Mary asked. "Yes ma'am, I had a 3.65 GPA. My high school coach said there is more to grades and swimming in life, if you keep a 3.5 and participate in sports and participate in life, then great things will happen. You can't be just one dimensional, or even two dimensional—be well rounded and enjoy college," Amy responded. "You must have had one heck of a leader in your coach, you were able to be an Academic All-American I see for all three seasons." "Yes ma'am, I was," Amy said with a big smile on her face.

"Terrific Amy, here at FarmPond we are very well rounded— each department has their own branches, and we expect all of our new employees to float from department to department in their first year— to develop them, so they are not one dimensional." "Yes, Mary—that sounds great. New teams, new people, new projects—yet still under the same umbrella," Amy said sitting up a little straighter. "Yes Amy, you've got it," Mary said, setting her coffee down.

"It says here that you went to Ireland," Mary asked. "Yes ma'am, I did—my junior year, because of my status at the engineering school. My professor, Professor Jones, without me knowing it, nominated me to study abroad for the spring semester. I won the nomination and was able to study at TriDub University. It was an amazing experience. New school, new friends, new country, and I even got to fly over the ocean for the first time. I volunteered at the student library, just to keep active and involved—didn't just want it to be school and study," Amy said very proudly.

"That is great Amy, here at FarmPond we have facilities in over forty-five countries, with processing plants in over seven—so traveling could be in your near future. We don't ask new employees to travel in their first year, but down the road we will ask you, as your career advances here," Mary explained. "Yes, that would be incredible!" said Amy with excitement.

"Amy, it says here that you were in a sorority," Mary stated. "Yes ma'am, I was, all four years. I loved it very much. Having moved here from out of state, I knew I needed to make friends, plus I wanted to be part of a sisterhood, much like I had with the swim team. Some of my upper classman teammates recommended that I rush, and so I did, and then joined one. I was even President of the sorority my senior year—I just loved the leadership I developed, and the unity of the house, it was something very special. It was a wonderful house, the social scene was great, homecoming, Moms' weekend, Dads' weekend, little sister weekend, and all the philanthropic work. It really was a lot of fun meeting alumni, the networking was terrific, and dear friends were created," Amy said with a note of confidence.

"Super, Amy, being a part of something at college, as you have done, really brings out the best in oneself—it's not just school, school, school—socializing, community involvement, allows one to prosper and grow wings to fly on your own down the road," Mary said. "Yes ma'am, I was nervous going to a new state, a new college—but because of my Mom and Dad's advice to get involved, not only swimming, I pushed myself to take on new challenges and test my strengths," Amy stated with a positive attitude.

"Amy, I really like your attitude on this—Frank told me you'd interview well." "Thank you, Mary, yes, a positive upbeat attitude and honesty is what I believe in," Amy responded with a smile of reassurance. "Great Amy, but hardships and setbacks hit individuals—please tell me a time you hit a wall but bounced back to overcome your challenge," Mary asked with a calmness over her, as if all set to hear her response. Amy took a sip of her coffee and set it down, "Yes, ma'am it was my sophomore year, I was not the fastest swimmer for the one-mile, and I moved to the number two slot. I just wasn't strong enough—so I talked to my coach, and he said if I could take 4 seconds off my time, then I would move back to number one. You'll be our top 1-mile swimmer again—my freshman year I was number 1 and half of my sophomore year, too. It was my fault I slipped in time, and in positioning. I was spending too much time in other places, trying to be so involved, so I had to drop a couple of my campus activities—going to all the home basketball games for starters. I limited myself to one a week, instead of three or four. I also dropped the school social club, where we planned the school activities for the month—meeting two times a week was too much. They understood. With those two decisions, I was able to regain my number 1 slot and beat my time by 5 seconds," Amy said in a proud voice.

"How'd that make you feel, Amy?" Mary asked, wanting to know more. "It felt really good to be back in the number 1 slot for the one-mile swim, that was the reason I was asked to come to State in the first place. The school recruited me because of my swimming and academic success, so I had to refocus on why I went to State—school and swim, and it was a good lesson for me, I can't do everything," Amy stated.

"Outstanding Amy, I like that approach. Your two internships look very interesting. One in Wyoming at a large ranch, where you tested soil samples and one in Florida, where you grew hybrid trees."

"Yes ma'am, both were very valuable for my engineering degree. I learned both sides of my degree, one in the field and one in the lab. One was six weeks, and one was eight weeks. But what I learned more about, was myself—the six-week program going into my junior year was paid for, the eight-week program going into my senior year paid me, but I had to pay my own living expenses, unlike the previous one— paying bills, budgeting, stretching a paycheck, and living within my means," Amy explained candidly.

"Amy, you nailed it, you didn't take the easy route, but you took the correct route for the result that you wanted. That result is this job at FarmPond, your background is what drove you to the top of our list. We interviewed over 175 candidates for this engineering position in the first round, and what you can bring to our company is what we are looking for—beyond just grades and major, your personality, your drive, your ethos is what places you at the top."

Mary went on to tell Amy, "FarmPond is a very sought-after company for college graduates, as well as for candidates working in other jobs. FarmPond is the elite engineering company in the world. Everyone wants to work here, but not everyone can. Investors love our company, shareholders love our company—we take our job very seriously, yet we have fun in what we do here. Like Frank told you at your first interview, there is more to landing the perfect job than just grades. It's working on a team, not being afraid to fail, stick-to-it-iv-ness, honesty, and being loyal to your fellow employees and management. Plus, the willingness to converse and laugh with others," Mary stated.

After over an hour, Mary told Amy that the final round of interviewing had concluded. Mary thanked Amy for coming in and told her that she was one of ten final candidates for the position of field engineer for FarmPond. Mary shook Amy's hand, walked her to the elevator, and said, "Thank you and good luck. We will call you within two days." Amy responded with, "Thank you Mary, and yes, I very much look forward to your phone call—have an amazing day."

With that Amy headed to her car, opened the door, sat down, closed the door, and put her head on the steering wheel and said, "Yes, I did it. I gave it all I had—if I get the job, awesome. If I don't, well I learned how to interview well for a second call back."

Amy made it home, gave Hank a big hug and kiss, called all her friends, and lastly, she called her parents. She said the interview went well and let the 48-hour wait begin—she looked forward to the fitness center tomorrow, seeing her work friends, seeing Sue, Jerry, and Tommy for pizza soon.

As she laid in bed, she said to herself—"I was the best me today."

Yes Amy, you were. You did awesome.......... Great job.

STOP

Flip the book over and read Jeff's tale.

If you have read both Amy and Jeff, turn the book around to Jeff's side, open to the gray pages and flip the book sideways

About Red Bike Publishing

Red Bike Publishing provides high quality books which can be found at www.redbikepublishing.com.

PUBLISHING

Get Rich in a Niche-The Insider's Guide to Self-Publishing in a Specialized Industry

OTHER TOPICS

1. Rainy Street Stories-Reflections on Secret Wars, Espionage and Terrorism
2. Around the Corner
3. 2000 Miles On Wisdom
4. Next in Line Please
5. Blue Jacket

NOVELS

1. Commitment-A Novel
2. Devoted

SECURITY BOOKS AND TRAINING

1. How to Get U.S. Government Contracts and Classified Work
2. Insider's Guide to Security Clearances

Other Books By Jim Serger

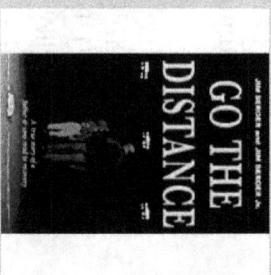

GO THE DISTANCE
JIM BERGER and JIM BERGER Jr.

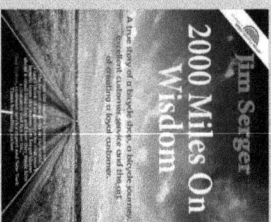

Jim Serger
2000 Miles On Wisdom

A true story of a bicycle shop, a bicycle journey of different customer service and the art of treating a loyal customer.

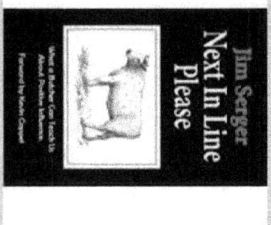

Jim Serger
Next In Line Please

What A Butcher Can Teach Us About Positive Influence

Foreword by Kevin Cognac

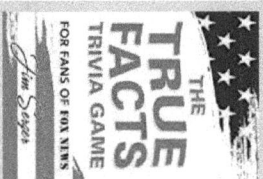

THE TRUE FACTS TRIVIA GAME
FOR FANS OF FOX NEWS

Jim Serger

is always on display. Leave a lasting, positive memory. Good luck to you and give them a reason to hire you.

A slew of interviews took place with Human Resources, and an interview with the head of sales, which lead to the final interview.

This college student, told me nearly a year later, why they were hired. After being advanced from Assistant Store Manager to Store Manager, the Regional Manager asked them, "Do you know why we hired you?" They replied, "Yes, it was my extensive resume." "Yes, you had an amazing resume, but so did the other candidate. The reason why we hired you, was because, you said yes." The Regional Manager told them.

A memorable experience. That is what the interview is, after you walk out the door. Positive or negative. An impression of you is created. The resume speaks for itself, that is why you got in the door. The one-on-one is where they will separate you from the others. So, give them a positive memory when you leave the interview. Something so simple as yes, just might be the one-percent separation that lands you the job.

One last item, for one-percent separation. Please clean up your voice mail message on your cellphone. A simple message will do, nothing over the top. Nothing flashy or catchy. Your true character

Getting The Call

Congratulations to Amy, for she has just landed the job. However, it was not easy. She went head-to-head with the most qualified candidates who applied for the open position. Candidates who had identical backgrounds, who presented themselves well on paper, and during the first couple waves of in-house interviewing. However, Amy, during the final interview, was separated based on one key word, the word yes. Yes, that little, tiny word separated her from Jeff, which landed Amy the position.

This story was shared with me, while I was a plant manager in the ice business. A young college student, whom I had the privilege of hiring and leading for three years, shared with me the reason why they were hired. This college student, before graduation, had applied for the position. Conducting interviews right before graduation and right after graduation. They said, it was a very rigorous process.

With that Mike sat down and said, "I guess we all know who we are going to hire." Mary said, "Amy it is. We have our new employee. Sadly, Jeff will never know that there was a possibility he would have been hired for a different position. It's unfortunate, but we do this interview process and gather information at this table for a reason. It's so all who engaged with the interviewees, have a say in who FarmPond brings on.... That's why we are the best team."

With that, Frank spoke, "In five months we will begin the search for our next best candidate."

Mike said, "I will go upstairs, and I will call Amy myself, and Frank you know what to do. Call Jeff and tell him good luck."

"I'd like to take this time to thank you all for what you bring to this table, your honesty and your abilities to look just beyond what seems to be perfect. Moreover, our abilities to work as a team," Mary said, as they cleaned up the conference room together.

That evening around 4:00 PM—Mike called Amy and offered her the position.

Jennifer went on to say, "Jeff looked great coming off the elevator. He was brawny, hair looked great, suit and tie perfect, however when he came over to my desk, he said, 'Yeah, I am Jeff. I am here to see the boss.' Right then and there I knew he was a cocky kid, someone who would not even say good afternoon to me. He was showing signs that he was better than me."

"And this is why Jennifer is always included in this process," Mary said. "If Jeff would not show respect for Jennifer, what is he going to do to the janitor, the cleaning lady, the delivery drivers, the dock workers—you all get the point?" Mike asked. "Yes," they all agreed.

Mary raised her hand, as she always did when she had something to add. Her co-workers always laughed. "Jennifer just reminded me of something so small, that I overlooked," Mary added. "Mary you and your hand raising, we know you have something great to say now," Mike said with a huge smile on his face. "Okay, okay, here I go. One thing to add about Amy and Jeff, to separate them both a little more, is the fact that one stood up and the other remained seated." "I don't understand," said Frank. "Well, Mike and I like to pop in on each other's interviews, and while I was seated with Amy, Mike came in and Amy stood up and shook his hand as I was introducing her to him. In return, in Jeff's interview when I came in, Jeff just stuck his hand out, not even standing up. He remained seated," Mary said with a frown.

Mary replied very quickly, "As a matter of fact I didn't realize it, but Amy was saying yes, she was saying no—it was such an elite interview, that the thought of saying the word yes, never even crossed my mind. Amy had a maturity to her tone. I took it for granted, never once saying to myself, wow this girl even says yes, till you brought it up. Amy spoke with respect, however I already explained that," Mary said with a shrugged shoulder motion.

Mike agreed, "Yes Mary, you did. Frank, what do you have to add?" "Not much to be honest with you, I never picked up on that in either candidate—I was honing in on their strengths, not even hearing the Yes or the Yeah—I knew their weaknesses, but one word or two words, I just did not pick up on those," Frank, said with big eyes, as he leaned back in his chair.

"Jennifer, you greeted both candidates, what did you gather?" Mary asked. "I did hear Amy say yes. She was very polite, and even asked how I was doing, and on the way out said nice to meet you, ma'am," Jennifer shared. "Great! See, for ten seconds, Jennifer explained Amy to a tee. Respectful," Mike said, and shared, "Amy was not there to impress Jennifer, yet still showed a sign of maturity and respect for her." Mary and Frank both agreed.

Mary proposed, "If we all feel that these two are the best of the best, what about moving up the field agent position? We could explain that a new position has just come open, we could move that slot up ninety days, and tell them we have a job which starts mid-September."

Mike said, a little louder than he intended, "Super idea, however in hearing what you all have to say about Amy, I have to add something that I picked up from Jeff. It's something that I wish wasn't there, and I could separate the candidates based on their resumes and backgrounds only. But it's something that I see all too often, and hearing it, made me cringe."

All at the table looked right at Mike, for Mike was about to bring something new to the table, a little kicker that no one else had brought up. Mike stood up and paced around the table, as if it had been on his mind the whole time. He paced, sipped some coffee, and proceeded to explain.

"Jeff, as strong of a candidate as he is, there was a hint of unprofessionalism, maybe a slight immaturity in him. It was that he always replied with, 'Yeah.' — 'Yeah, Mike.' — 'Yeah, I can do that.' 'Yeah, thanks for having me today.' Yeah, Yeah, Yeah and even a few Nope, Nope, Nope. It was never a Yes or a No—it was yeah. Did anyone else pick up on that?" Mike said with a big question mark over his head.

"Jeff is a true leader," Mike said emphatically. With this bold statement, all the heads at the table nodded yes simultaneously. "Jeff, without a doubt, is the line leader, his mannerisms, during our time, were that of a gentleman and scholar. He, too, drank his coffee while engaging in conversation, and sat up straight, and had a firm handshake, and made eye contact." Mike proceeded with his rave review.

"Jeff is incredibly well-rounded and was so upbeat and positive in his interview. This young man has already participated in so many aspects of life, and he's only 22. He worked while in college, was on the baseball team, had internships, and studied abroad. He was on an academic scholarship to PolyTech, and when I spoke with his references, they, too, talked about Jeff exactly the way Jeff presented himself in the meeting," Mike explained.

"Hearing that, he sounds very similar to Amy," Mary added to the conversation. "Yes, it is going to be difficult to hire just one, and remember we will need to hire another field agent in about six months. That six months will fly by, and we will have to go through this entire process again, and boy is it ever time consuming, but we must hire the best, to be the best," Mike said with a big sigh.

Mary went on to explain, "Amy was able to keep the conversation going, asking questions, listening to my answers, and asking follow-up questions. Even telling little tid bits of her personal life, to fill in the cracks of how she might fit in at FarmPond. She understood failure, she understood setbacks, and she overcame them." "Setbacks—Yes, now that is a young lady who is not afraid of failure," Mike said. They all smiled. Frank replied, "Yes, she told me she loved to try new things, and sometimes they worked and sometimes they didn't. She told me that at least she gave it her best shot." "Sounds like a solid candidate, she knows her limits, but isn't afraid to try something new, or adapt and overcome," Mike said. The Marine in him was pleased.

Mary dove into a little more explaining, how Amy had traveled for internships, studied abroad, and most of all and what she really thought was a keen trait, was Amy's determination to keep her grades up while working on her engineering degree and staying very involved in all aspects of school. "Yes, outstanding," said Mike.

"Mike, why don't you tell us about Jeff, it seems we all agree that Amy is a very strong candidate," Mary said with excitement, looking forward to hearing about Mike's interview. "Yes, of course—I am in awe of what Amy could bring to FarmPond, seems like she would be an excellent addition," Mike ended.

as if soaking all of what I was saying into her brain to produce an intelligent answer." The others nodded their heads to show they agreed with her. Mary went on, "Amy actually sipped her coffee, she was not shy, she was engaging as if we were old friends meeting up for a little coffee—she was very relaxed, confident and radiant—she was giving off the at-home feeling, as if she had been working alongside us for years." Mike said, "Great to hear that." Mary went on to say, "Amy was really going into detail about how she knew her neighbors' names, how she met new people every day at her fitness center, and how she loved to lead the campus tours." "Now that is a young lady who has leadership skills," Frank chimed in. "Yes, it is clear she has skills in communication, leadership, and teamwork," Mike said. "Yes, she does," Mary said. "Strong skills. In listening to her, she spoke highly of her parents, and she spoke a little of her sister, which gave me the notion that she has great love for and a solid relationship with her family. Also, she stated that she always gets together with her friends, so she understands the need for friendship. She said she calls her parents every day to check in." "Her parents seem like strong leaders too, leaders producing leaders," Mike said. They all nodded in agreement. Mary added, "And the kicker is, she talked about visiting her grandparents each time she was home from college." "Nice," said Mike. "That is very nice."

to tell their friends and parents, however deep down inside they are comfortable with the college life, a new routine is just out of their league, so they will make up a story about us to cover their tracks. It's all good, that's just how real life works—I am just glad they didn't waste your time in person, Frank," Mike concluded. "Me too," said Mary.

Mike said, "Well folks, we had over 175 college graduates apply for this job. Per FarmPond protocol, we screened them with the online process, screened them on paper, screened them with a phone interview, and Frank met several in person. Then from there we whittled it down to our two best candidates. Mary interviewed one and I interviewed the other. Due to our high standards, we reel in the best of the best. We only have one position and that is why we are here today. Two candidates, and I feel that either one of them would be a great addition to our company. Last Tuesday we had fifteen candidates to go over, we did an excellent job at bringing forth their best assets, and we did a terrific job at pinpointing their weaknesses, and why they wouldn't be a great fit here."

"Okay, here I go," Mary dove right in. "Amy was just like Frank explained to us last week. Firm handshake, eye contact, and she sat up straight in her interview. She attentively listened to my questions, then she would respond, she was not interrupting halfway through—she allowed me to finish, have someone else go over it, and at least look up the guidelines on how to write a resume, other candidates would have been considered to interview—but, you only get one crack at this. Frank, you've done this for a long time, we appreciate how you weeded them out. Great job." Mary smiled. "Yes Frank, good job. We really appreciate your high standards of excellence," said Mike.

Frank went on, "Beyond the ones that never made it into our building, there were many others I weeded out immediately upon meeting them. They would not make eye contact, they didn't shake my hand, they rambled on and on about their grades, they rambled on and on about their school activities, as if they were an individual. Many of them never once spoke on team or teamwork. It was all about them," Frank said. "Yes, just an individual, just so into themselves, and not giving credit to others—me, me, me," said Mike. "It's sad to say, but those folks have tremendous backgrounds I am sure, yet such me thinkers." Mike went on. Mary agreed, once again telling Frank, "Great job pinpointing those little flaws, they could lead to big flaws. I don't mind coaching young kids, however if they are that self-absorbed in the first interview, then we don't want them."

Frank proceeded to explain that a few candidates never even returned his phone call to have a first interview. "I am not surprised at all," said Mike quickly. "They want the job on paper, they want the job

The very next day, which was preplanned—Mary, Mike, and Frank, as well as the receptionist, Jennifer, were to meet in the first-floor conference room at 10:00 a.m. Coffee and bagels would be provided, and if the meeting lasted longer than two hours, lunch would be ordered. They all knew it was going to be a lengthy meeting, lobbying back and forth, vouching for their candidate, and expressing what they had learned from each candidate.

Mike opened the conversation with, "Well folks, that was a very intense few days, I am very excited for our candidates and to hear your feedback on each one of them. Frank why don't you go first, Mary and I will finish it up, then Jennifer will add anything she may have picked up—then we will choose our best candidate."

Frank started with, "Wow, their backgrounds. What I picked up first from their resumes, and why we called them in was how neat and clean both resumes were. From an HR perspective, I can't begin to tell you how many graduates we passed on just because on paper they didn't present themselves well. Misspelled words, no email at the bottom provided, like we asked. Some didn't list any past activities, just their college attendance—as if four years were the only years they had lived." Mary chimed in, "I know what you mean, your first mark of impressing is the resume—if you take your time, proofread it,

STOP

Flip book over and read Amy's tale

If you have read both Amy and Jeff, turn to the next page, flip the book sideways and read the gray pages.

As he laid in bed, he said to himself—"I was the best me today."

Yeah Jeff, you were. You did awesome.......... Great job.

Mike went on to tell Jeff, "FarmPond is a very sought-after company for college graduates, as well as for candidates working in other jobs. FarmPond is the elite engineering company in the world. Everyone wants to work here, but not everyone can. Investors love our company, shareholders love our company—we take our job very seriously, yet we have fun in what we do here. Like Frank told you at your first interview, there is more to landing the perfect job than just grades. It's working on a team, not being afraid to fail, stick-to-it-iv-ness, honesty, and being loyal to your fellow employees and management. Plus, the willingness to converse and laugh with others," Mike stated.

After over an hour, Mike told Jeff that the final round of interviewing had concluded. Mike thanked Jeff for coming in and told him that he was one of ten final candidates for the position of field engineer for FarmPond. Mike shook Jeff's hand walked him to the elevator, and said, "Thank you and good luck. We will call you within two days." Jeff responded with, "Thanks Mike, and yeah, I very much look forward to your phone call—have an amazing day."

With that Jeff headed to his car, opened the door, sat down, closed the door, and put his head on the steering wheel and said, "Yeah, I did it. I gave it all I had—if I get the job, awesome. If I don't, well I learned how to interview well for a second call back."

Jeff made it home, gave Zeus a big hug, called all his friends, and lastly, he called his parents. He said the interview went well and let the 48-hour wait begin—he looked forward to the fitness center tomorrow, seeing his work friends, seeing Mark, Michelle, and Hannah for pizza soon.

"How'd that make you feel, Jeff?" Mike asked, wanting to know more. "It felt really good to be placing the bat on the ball, moving runners around, that was the reason I was asked to come to PolyTech in the first place. The school recruited me to play baseball and also for my academic status, so I had to refocus on why I went to PolyTech—school and ball, and it was a good lesson for me. I can't do everything," Jeff stated.

"Outstanding Jeff, I like that approach. Your two internships look very interesting. One in Nevada on the lake, where you tested water samples and one in Louisiana where you helped work on a reverse osmosis at a water treatment plant." "Yeah Mike, both were very valuable for my engineering degree. I learned both sides of my degree, one in the field and one in the plant. One was six weeks, and one was eight weeks, but what I learned more about was myself—the six-week program going into my junior year was paid for, the eight-week program going into my senior year paid me, but I had to pay my own living expenses, unlike the previous one—paying bills, budgeting, stretching a paycheck, and living within my means," Jeff explained candidly.

"Jeff, you nailed it, you didn't take the easy route, but you took the correct route for the result that you wanted. That result is this job at FarmPond, your background is what drove you to the top of our list. We interviewed over 175 candidates for this engineering position in the first round, and what you can bring to our company is what we are looking for—beyond just grades and major, your personality, your drive, your ethos is what places you at the top."

"Jeff, I really like your attitude on this—Frank told me you'd interview well." "Thanks, Mike. Yeah, a positive upbeat attitude and honesty is what I believe in," Jeff responded with a smile of reassurance. "Great Jeff, but hardships and setbacks hit individuals—please tell me a time you hit a wall but bounced back to overcome your challenge," Mike asked with a calmness over him, as if all set to hear his response. Jeff took a sip of his coffee and set it down, "Yeah, it was my sophomore year, I was not connecting with the ball well. I moved from the number 3 hitter to the number 8 hitter. I just wasn't seeing the ball—so I talked to my coach, and he said if I could put in the time, the hitting coach and he would do some one-on-one drills to develop my bat speed and eye contact. Then maybe, I'd move back up in the batting order. He said I'd be driving them in, hitting again. My freshman year I was number seven and for a hand full of games my sophomore year number three—It was my fault I slipped in the lineup. I was spending too much time in other places, trying to be so involved, so I had to drop a couple of my campus activities—going to all the home lacrosse games for the girls and boys for starters. I limited myself to one a week, instead of three or four. I also dropped the school social club, where we planned the school activities for the month—meeting two times a week was too much. They understood. With those two choices, I was able to hit the batting cages more often, and hit off the tee, as well as have instructional time with my coaches. The payoff was my batting average went up, runs batted in went up, and I moved to number five, right behind the cleanup batter," Jeff said in a proud voice.

"That is great Jeff, here at FarmPond we have facilities in over forty-five countries, with processing plants in over seven—so traveling could be in your near future. We don't ask new employees to travel in their first year, but down the road we will ask you, as your career advances here," Mike explained. "Yeah, that would be incredible!" said Jeff with excitement.

"Jeff, it says here that you were in a fraternity," Mike asked. "Yeah, I was. All four years. I loved it very much. Having moved here from out of state, I knew I needed to make friends, plus I wanted to be a part of a brotherhood much like I had with the baseball team—some of my upper classman teammates recommended that I rush, and so I did, and then joined one. I was President of the fraternity my senior year—I just loved the leadership I developed, and the unity of the house, it was something very special. It was a wonderful house, the social scene was great, homecoming, Moms' weekend, Dads' weekend, little brother weekend, and all the philanthropic work—It really was a lot of fun meeting alumni, the networking was terrific, and awesome friends were created," Jeff said with a note of confidence.

"Super, Jeff, being a part of something at college, as you have done, really brings out the best in oneself—it's not just school, school, school—socializing, community involvement, allows one to prosper and grow wings to fly on your own down the road," Mike said. "Yeah, I was nervous going to a new state, a new college—but because of my Mom and Dad's advice to get involved, not only baseball, I pushed myself to take on new challenges and test my strengths," Jeff stated with a trainable attitude.

open position, and campus gave me a floating schedule, so I was able to work 10 to 30 hours a week, when not swinging the bat."

"Oh, that's great Jeff—did your grades keep up?" Mike asked. "Yeah, I had a 3.65 GPA. My high school coach said there is more to grades and playing ball in life, if you keep a 3.5 and participate in sports and participate in life, then great things will happen. You can't be just one dimensional, or even two dimensional—be well rounded and enjoy college," Jeff responded. "You must have had one heck of a leader in your coach, you were able to be an Academic All-American I see for all three seasons." "Yeah, I was," Jeff said with a big smile on his face.

"Terrific Jeff, here at FarmPond we are very well rounded—each department has their own branches to it, and we expect all of our new employees to float from department to department in their first year— to develop them, so they are not one dimensional." "Yeah, Mike—that sounds great. New teams, new people, new projects—yet still under the same umbrella," Jeff said sitting up a little straighter. "Yes Jeff, you've got it," Mike said, setting his coffee down.

"It says here that you went to England," Mike asked. "Yeah, I did—my junior year, because of my status at the engineering school. My professor, Professor Doyle, without me knowing it, nominated me to study abroad for the spring semester. I won the nomination and was able to study at the University of Merrillville. It was such an amazing experience. New school, new friends, new country, and I even got to fly over the ocean for the first time. I volunteered at the student union, just to keep active and involved—didn't just want it to be school and study," Jeff said very proudly.

parents, I landed funny and tore my ACL, but through rehab my knee is fine—But, I had to give up baseball, the twisting and turning was just too much, however I was able to stay on as a manager of the team for my senior year. It stung not to play, but I still had my teammates and finished out my final season as part of the team, still continuing to offer my services anyway I could. Additionally, I was able to keep my co-captain status."

"Very good, Jeff! Team—that's what our business is about," Mike said with gusto. "Yeah, Mike I love team—like coach said, Together Everyone Achieves More," Jeff shared with zest. "Yes Jeff, no individualism here—we are all a team," Mike replied, showing Jeff he is a part of the team as well, not just a leader.

"Jeff, I'd like to hear about Central America," Mike asked inquisitively. "Yeah, at the end of my freshman year I wanted to find an internship, but due to my freshman status no one would take me on, so I contacted my church, and they were able to set me up with a local charity that helped set up schools in Central America. My pastor helped me because I had been involved in after school activities with children, with my family and friends since 4th grade—I landed the opportunity, and the PolyTech college fitness center was able to give me three weeks off, to go down and volunteer. It was a wonderful experience." Jeff was so proud of the kinship he developed down there.

"Your PolyTech college fitness center, what is that?" asked Mike with a hint of wonder. "When I was a freshman, I wanted to be involved more with the college, not just play ball, but also work on campus. I was living in the dorms, at the time, and I wanted to make more friends and have a little spending money, too. I applied for the

the city," Jeff stated, with a Christmas card worthy smile. A calmness came over Jeff, after hearing Mike's words.

Mike and Jeff proceeded to sit down in two leather chairs with a small glass table between them. There on the table was Jeff's resume, as well as two coffee cups and a small pot. "Would you like some coffee?" Mike asked, "Or would you like a glass of water?" "Yeah, coffee is fine, thanks," Jeff said. Then a small conversation commenced, and after two minutes of friendly chit chat Mike asked Jeff a starter question, that Jeff didn't see coming. "Have you ever watched an Army Navy football game?"—Jeff responded right away, "Yeah, I have." "I think the game brings out the best in both schools," said Mike. "Yeah, me too—I remember watching the game and thinking that these players, from all around the country, are going to a prestigious military academy, and are playing as a unit," Jeff said. "Why yes, I've thought that, too. I like the fact that the teams are competing against each other, yet they both have one mission in the end. They will defend our country as a unit," Mike said with excitement. "Yeah," Jeff said with a bit of enthusiasm. "Yes, super committed soldiers and sailors," Mike said with a smile of admiration on his face.

Suddenly, Jeff was at ease, very relaxed, as if meeting up with his cycling buddies. He thought, I guess that was the question— "Yeah, I nailed it," Jeff thought to himself. Mike, with a sip of his coffee, hunkered down and dove right into the interview.

"I see you were on the baseball team," Mike stated. "Yeah, my freshman, sophomore and junior years," Jeff said with confidence. "But I had to pull out due to a knee injury I suffered in the spring. Yeah, you see I was skiing while vacationing with my brother and

With two minutes to spare, Jeff gave Zeus a pat on the back, and was in the car at 1:30 p.m.—right on time and headed out for FarmPond. Jeff hit every single red light, however because he left early, he arrived in the parking garage at 2:40. He looked himself over in the mirror one more time, and with one last lint brush roll he proceeded to walk up to the lobby—hit the elevator button, stepped in, and spun around with a smile from ear to ear. He hit the 6th floor button—the door closed, one big deep breath and the door opened, with a nod of confidence he stepped out and proceeded to the receptionist desk. "Hey, I am Jeff, I have a 3 o'clock appointment with the boss."— "Yes Jeff, please have a seat and Mike will be right with you."— "Yeah, thank you," Jeff replied with a rush of excitement over him.

Jeff took a seat on the leather chair overlooking the city—"What a view," he said to himself. "Nice to meet you." "Hello." "Thank you." "Handshake."—all racing through Jeff's thoughts—another big deep breath was needed to calm him down, then he said to himself—"Jeff, be the best YOU." "Jeff," the receptionist said. "Yeah," Jeff said. "Mike will see you now." With that, Jeff stood up, smile on, the receptionist opened the huge mahogany wood doors with solid brass handles and there right in front of him about fifteen feet away was Mike standing up behind his glass desk, with books, awards, and certificates displayed on his back shelves.

Mike stepped out from around his desk and met Jeff halfway— the two shook hands, "Jeff, it is so nice to finally meet you. I am Mike Wilson. I have read over all of your accomplishments, and Frank has told me wonderful things about you." "Yeah Mike, very nice to meet you as well, what an amazing office you have and what a terrific view of take the edge off—it worked. Mark looked over Jeff's suit and tie, "You're set," he said. "You're going to look great and be great," Mark stated with a rush of excitement. They mapped out how far of a drive it was—55 minutes, so they agreed that he should leave an hour and half early—1:30, allowing 60 minutes for red lights, traffic, or whatever may be out of the norm. Arrive in the garage, go over a few things, then walk up and be in the lobby at 2:50.

Monday 7:00 alarm was beeping, Jeff leashed up Zeus—morning stroll was complete, fed Zeus, morning eggs and bacon complete, morning cup of joe done. He put on some street clothes and took Zeus for a 1-mile walk—burn off some energy. Back at the apartment, Jeff looked over his suit, tie, and shoes. "Check, Check, Check." Jeff was still a bit hyper with excitement. He looked in the mirror above his dresser— "Hey, I am Jeff, very nice to meet you sir." "Hey, I am Jeff, great to see you sir."— "Hey, I am Jeff, good afternoon, sir, thanks for having me."

It was only 8:30 and Jeff's brain was starting to run—so he said, "I need a 45-minute workout, exercise is good for the brain coach always said." With that, Jeff was at ease, his go-to-routine never fails, indoor spinning. At 10:30, he took Zeus on one last quick stroll and got ready to go. 11:50, Jeff had showered, and was dressed for success, hair perfect, shoes spit shined, and with one last look in the mirror—his phone rang, it was Mom. "Jeff, I just wanted to say how much I love you, be yourself and enjoy this moment, you deserve it." "Yeah, Thanks Mom, I love you, too—I'll call you the moment it's over." "Okay dear— just be you." "Yeah, Mom—got to go, I love you."

listen thoughtfully, and respond, really pay attention, different than the kind of listening he did with his friends. Jeff understood and they practiced over a few slices of pizza. Mark, also, tossed a couple questions his way. Jeff responded well, then they laughed and laughed. Knowing that Jeff was as ready as ever.

Friday came and went fast. Friday night, he laid out his suit and tie for the interview, and once again went over his past accomplishments. Saturday, he worked a half-day, 11:00-3:00, and met up with Mark, Michelle, and Hannah as well as others at a Hannah's house for a small party, as they normally did over the weekend. The house rotated each weekend. Everyone was so excited for Jeff. Michelle, who Jeff dated off and on for part of his freshman and sophomore years, was Jeff's best friend, that was a girl, and she was so happy for him—saying over and over that he deserved the very best, and FarmPond was going to get the best. Hannah and he met after she transferred over from another college. They were in the engineering department together and worked in the lab together off and on. Everyone gave him hugs, gave him congratulations, but Jeff said, "The verdict is still out. Monday at three o'clock will be the deciding factor."

Sundays Jeff normally didn't have to work, however his boss, Randy, was able to switch Jeff's schedule to allow him off on Monday for the interview. Jeff hated to work Sundays, but this Sunday he was happy to be there. It was only a half-day, so he knew it would fly by. He just needed to do his work, keep his normal work routine, and he'd be home soon. Mark was coming over at 4:00 p.m., it was a guys' evening. Burgers on the grill, watch some baseball, put Jeff at ease,

That night after 6:00 p.m., he called his mom and dad—respecting that his dad was a high school teacher, and his mom was an interior designer—he knew they couldn't talk at three—school letting out and Mom being occupied—so 6:00 p.m. was a good time to call and share the great news. He told them all about it, "Monday at 3:00 p.m., downtown." His mom and dad repeated themselves over and over like a broken record, "We love you, and we are so proud of you." Just like they have always done his whole life. Dad gave a little more advice than normal, like most dads do—knowing that Mom was just so nervous and excited. Dad playing the cool and calm role explained to Jeff, that FarmPond didn't just call anyone back, they called him. "You are awesome and will bring so much passion to FarmPond." Jeff said, "Yeah thanks," and believed his dad was right. Dad and Mom simultaneously said, "We love you, Jeff." "Yeah, I love you both too and thanks for always supporting me."

Jeff knew Thursday was going to be a great day—sleep in a little if he could. A Zeus doggy road trip, pizza with Mark, a good workout, bike for sure, and most of all, plan his attack, and attack his plan for the interview.

On Friday, same routine as normal for a workday, 11:00-6:00, then right home. He thought to himself. But it's Thursday, his day to get things done, then a slice and a beer with Mark. Mark has been his sidekick and friend since day one four years ago in the dorm. That night Mark and he went over his resume, highlighting the strengths that Jeff had to offer, and weaknesses that he could work toward adjusting. Jeff loved to talk, so Mark reminded him to focus on Mike's questions, listen, then respond. No guessing on what Mike had to say, jumping up and down now, was shouting, "They called me back! They called me back!" Randy gave him a huge high-five, and a punch on his shoulder. He knew Jeff deserved this second interview—Jeff calmed down, but still radiated pure glee, he resumed his station and waited until 3:00 p.m. to tell anyone—that's the respect Jeff had for his employers, and why FarmPond called him back. He was committed.

At three on the dot, he sprinted all the way home—jumping over puddles, curbs, and even jaywalking to get home. New record, 5:45—15 seconds faster than the day before. The sun was shining. He unlocked the door and gave Zeus the biggest hug, and they danced a little in the kitchen. He took him out and back in, fed him, and proceeded to call Mark to tell him all about it.

Mark said, "We still on for pizza tomorrow night?" "Of course, yeah we are," Jeff said at the top of his lungs. And at the same time the guys yelled, "Awesome!" Jeff said, "What do I wear for the interview? Black shoes or brown shoes, red power tie, or blue shirt, buttoned down collar or should I wear a three-piece suit." "Slow down Jeff, slow down. We will go over all of that over pizza," Mark said in a reassuring voice. "See you then Mark. 6 o'clock, peace out." Click....

Thursdays Jeff does not have to work, for that is his laundry day, grocery day, ironing day, get things done day and most important, spend time one-on-one with Zeus day. He normally took him down to the tiny river that runs around downtown. He dipped into the water, they played fetch, and he got to carry around sticks in his mouth. Big day for Zeus and Jeff—they usually even got an ice-cream for the ride home. So, he said right to Zeus' face, "We are keeping our special day tomorrow."

said as his first patron came in, "Okay, thanks have a super workout." As he always said after confirming they were affiliated with the school.

About 35 minutes into his routine, his phone rang, and it was a phone number that he did recognize. "Hello, this is Jeff."— "Jeff, this is Frank from FarmPond, how are you today?" With that Jeff smiled from ear to ear and hit the help button which was a direct line for Randy to come to his assistance. "Yeah Sir, I am well—I have been looking forward to this phone call." "Great Jeff, and I am so happy to call you, as well. We would love for you to come in for a final interview, which will be with our Senior Vice President, Mike Wilson. Does Monday at 3:00 p.m. work for you?" "Yeah, it does," Jeff said with a crackle of excitement in his voice. "Monday at 3:00 p.m. is perfect, I really appreciate the opportunity Frank, it means the world to me." "Jeff, we look forward to seeing you. Park in the garage like you did before, take the stairs to the lobby, then, take the elevator to the 6th floor—not 5th for me, but 6th for Mike Wilson. The receptionist will greet you, and she will take you in for the interview." "Yeah Frank, that sounds good. I look forward to Monday," Jeff said, with a smile so big that everyone in the fitness center could see him gleaming with joy. "Okay Jeff, we will see you at 3:00 p.m. on Monday, have a terrific weekend," Frank said, with a hint of joy in his voice. "Yeah, thank you Sir, I will—you as well, and thanks for calling. You've made my week." "Good-bye Jeff." "See you Frank."

Randy, who had taken over Jeff's station while he was on the phone, also had a huge smile and jumped up out of his seat, seeing how Jeff's eyes were glazed over, he was red in the face, and he had a slight stare of amazement. Randy knew Jeff had received the call. Jeff,

Professor Doyle said it would—even a little rumble in the distance could be heard. Zeus was startled a few times, but with the morning came just a few sprinkles—the heavy stuff must have come and gone in the middle of the night.

Jeff hooked up Zeus –quick out and to the point, he hated the rain. Back in, fed him, and he started his eggs and pre-cooked bacon routine. Today Jeff's schedule at work was a half-day, he was only in from 11:00-3:00. "Can't get these kids into overtime," he laughed to himself knowing that big things were on the horizon. Workout, "Check!" He yelled out when done, took a quick shower, and headed off to campus.

As he opened the door, he touched the sign on the way out and said, "Today is the day, I will hear back from them." He popped open his umbrella and took off with a quick pace to campus. A little drizzle, and a few puddles which he zig-zagged around like he was catching a fly ball—quick and fast—as he approached the Center, he could see the sun trying to peek through, as if a sign to him of good things to come.

Arriving fifteen minutes early, as he always did, Jeff grabbed his clipboard and was off to the front desk. Today, since it was a short day, he would just check IDs for two hours and lifeguard his last two. As he maintained his station, his boss Randy asked if he had heard anything from the Farm, yet. Jeff stated, "Nope." Randy, in a mentor voice, said, "Jeff, if you need anything at all please ask me and I'll do my best to help you." "I really appreciate that, Randy," Jeff replied, knowing that he was a PolyTech athlete and worked with the school since graduating a few years back. Jeff knew Randy always rooted for him—just had to be the boss first and a leader and mentor second. "ID please," Jeff times, and to campus activities. Mr. Martin was kind of a dad away from home. "Have you heard anything from that company you interviewed with?" "Nope, not yet," said Jeff. "Good things come to good people, and you're good people," Mr. Martin said with a hearty tone. "Yeah, thank you Mr. Martin. If you need anything let me know and have a great night." "You too, Jeff," Mr. Martin said, and "Thank you, for helping me so much." Jeff said, "No problem. I've got to go grab Zeus." "Yes Zeus, go, go, go I'll talk with you later," Mr. Martin said and pointed to the door... "Go, Go, Go."

Jeff grabbed Zeus and headed down to the Bark Park—routine in check, then back to the apartment—texting and talking with his parents along the way. Nothing new to share with them, however his parents showered him with support, as well as sharing that Grandma and Grandpa were so proud of him, too. His brother even texted to tell him to keep the eye on the prize, normal brother quick text. He was busy at his own college; he was a sophomore, having fun and keeping his grades up with all his activities. Big brother influence was working.

Jeff nodded off to sleep, eyes closed, eyes open, eyes closed, eyes open all night—could be the humidity, it was high, grey clouds were rolling in and the scent of rain was in the air. "Professor Doyle was right—it is going to rain," Jeff thought. With that, his eyes closed, and stayed closed.

Jeff tossed and turned all night long—he glanced at the clock, 1:00 a.m., 4:00 a.m., and finally at 6:30 a.m. his alarm went off. Even Zeus, all night long was on the bed and off the bed, on the bed, off the bed. A small tapping at his window could be heard—now he understood why he didn't sleep well—it had started to rain, just like

At 6:30 p.m., after conversing with his fellow staffers and students, he was out the door and once again, as it always happened, he ran into Professor Doyle. Today Professor Doyle threw something his way, which he had heard a million times, "Are you being the best you today?" "Yeah, Professor Doyle, I am the best me today." "Very good, keep it up. It is supposed to rain tomorrow, more reason to be the best you." "Yeah," stated Jeff. As Professor Doyle crossed the street she called back, "Have a super evening, Jeff." "You too, Professor Doyle."

"Why did she tell me it was going to rain," Jeff wondered aloud, but that was Professor Doyle, no matter how bad things might get, be the best you. He smiled and sprinted all the way home. New record, 6 minutes in an all-out sprint. His best time was 6:45—he knocked off 45 seconds, must have been Professor Doyle's pep talk, or that all the lights had the walk sign, he laughed. As he approached his front door his phone rang, it was a number that was not familiar. His heart raced.

Jeff answered the phone right away, "Hello." "Your car warranty is about to expire," said the computer-generated voice. With that, Jeff hung up and a slight smirk and laugh came over him, just then his neighbor popped into the hallway and said, "Hi Jeff." He said, "Yeah, hello there Mr. Martin." Mr. Martin had lived in the apartment complex forever, a retired PolyTech Professor, who loved Poly so much, that he consistently gave his time volunteering at the PolyTech hospital for children. He read to the kids three times a week for a few hours. They adored him. He had been a terrific neighbor to Jeff, and Jeff, being good hearted had watched over him, too. He checked on him when the weather was bad and had taken him to the store a few for Thursday. "Of course, YEAH Mark, I will be there, and I hope to share with you some great news." Mark stated, "Jeff, if they don't hire you, they are morons." Jeff responded upbeat, "I know Mark, I understand, however it's a big company, but I gave my best interview, so I just know they will call me back, I just know they will." Mark, who was feeling very protective, said, "If they don't, I'll go down there myself and tell them what's what. I've been taking Aikido and I'm not afraid to use it!" Jeff started laughing and soon Mark was laughing, too. Laughter was a big part of their friendship. So many great times and the best of friends, always having each other's back. Jeff said, "Yeah Mark, you'll show them who's boss." With that pep talk, Jeff had to get ready for work— "Check you later, Mark."— "Adios Jeff, make it a great day." Jeff got ready for work and took Zeus out for one more short walk, and at 10:30 was out the door. He touched the sign with his right hand saying to himself, "There is only one of you, be the best you."

Today was a different day for Jeff at the campus fitness center— he was the tour guide from 11:00-1:00 for potential students. He loved this day, for one day a week he could share his passion and school spirit for Polytech with students who might attend in the fall. He loved to lead a group, loved to answer questions—for his knowledge of the school was on display, and the visitors felt it. From 1:00-3:00, Jeff worked the phones, and from 3:30-6:00 Jeff was the facility safety officer, making his rounds so students understood how to use the equipment correctly and safely. He also made sure the facility grounds were orderly and neat. He always said cheerfully, "If you need help, please just ask. My name is Jeff."

those words carved into it. It hangs on the wall to the right of his front door. As he heads out, those words "There is only one of you, be the best you" are what he carries with him and strives to live by each day.

Jeff made it home quick, fed Zeus, and cooked up his evening meal, or the normal go to meal when nothing was planned, ramen noodles. He sat in his comfortable recliner, which he had purchased at the local thrift shop a few years back, and ate his dinner. He watched a little television, no cable but just local channels—Jeff wanted to save money, plus he wasn't that into television. Jeff was into biking. After his meal settled, Jeff got the mountain bike down, and headed out to meet up with a couple of buddies. Jeff had been in a bike club since freshman year in the dorm. Half of his floor was in on it, which gave the guys a reason to get together every week to talk, laugh, and bounce ideas off each other—plus hit the paths of the local community. Biking was huge in college for Jeff. Only now it was down to just three guys— but three close friends, who got along so well. Three friends that Jeff knew would be lasting buddies.

By the end of the evening, Jeff had texted or received phone calls from numerous people, including Mom and Dad, who wanted to know about FarmPond. Mom was so worried, asking question after question and Dad was so excited too, giving him his dad speech, which was just a ring-side manager pep talk. He loved them both so much.

By 11:00 p.m. Jeff was off to bed, hoping that tomorrow would be the big day. At 7:00 a.m. the alarm went off, and Jeff was up and at it. Zeus was out, morning meal down the hatch, and 45-minute workout complete, this time it was yoga. On cue, he received his normal call from Mark about FarmPond and confirmed their dinner with a big smile, and blushing yelled over, "Thanks a bunch, see you over the weekend."

By 10:45 Jeff was in the building all set and ready for his 7-hour shift—which included life guarding from 11:00-1:00, weight room monitoring student IDs from 1:00-3:00, a little 30-minute break for lunch, and from 3:30 till 6:00 Jeff oversaw student photos, data entry, and answered the campus fitness room's phone. Jeff loved it, the friends he made because of landing this job were unbelievable, and he was very aware that he only had two weeks left.

He graduated just three weeks back, May 15th to be exact. Jeff loved college life, but his four years at PolyTech were ending soon—for Jeff to stay on at the campus Fitness Center, he would have to enroll in fall classes and work on his Master's Degree. However, Jeff knew he needed to hit the work force, and work on his Master's in the future after he had a few years of real-life experience under his belt. FarmPond was just the company to gain that experience. He was ready for the call.

Jeff left the Center around 6:30 p.m. His colleagues and he would, joke, have a few laughs, and talk about the day before he would walk back home. On the way home, Jeff usually ran into his former freshman Business 101 Professor, Professor Doyle. They would stop, and talk for five minutes or so, and she would remind him, just as she always did his freshman year, "There is only one of you, be the best you."

Jeff loved that quote by Professor Doyle. He loved it so much that for his college graduation present his parents, who had heard it so many times over the last four years, gave him a wooden plaque with for their usual one-mile morning walk. Once back at the apartment, Zeus jumped up on the couch and settled down for his morning nap and Jeff began to spin on his indoor bike. After 45 minutes or so Jeff stopped, drenched in sweat, and began his cool down, when his phone rang.

Mark, his great college friend, called to see how he was and to check if FarmPond had called him back. Jeff said, "Nope." Mark understood it was only day eight. Mark asked if he wanted to have dinner on Thursday night after work. Jeff replied, "Yeah, of course I do." So, their normal mid-week get together was lined up at the local pizza dive on Long Oak Street right by campus. "Love you man," Mark said. "Back at yeah," Jeff replied, and he said, "I'll text you later. I have to be at work in about an hour."

Four years ago, at freshman orientation, Jeff learned about the various jobs available on campus. Jeff, being athletic and outgoing, was in the Student Fitness Center on the campus tour when the guide stated that college students could work a few hours a week at various campus spots—the cafeteria, the library, the bookstore, the student union, and the on-campus fitness building.

Jeff was showered and ready to go to his job—the same job he had off and on in college, depending on the semester. Jeff was able to walk there from his apartment, just a little over a half a mile, but living on campus his freshman and sophomore year it was just a hop, skip and a jump. Walking to work Jeff usually ran into a few fellow students. Today Michelle yelled from the other side of the street, "Did you get the job?" Jeff replied, "I haven't heard back." With that, Michelle's friend yelled over, "You've got this Jeff, hang in there." Jeff

Jeff's Tale

It had been over a week since Jeff had his first interview with FarmPond. As he exited the interview, Frank, from FarmPond Human Resources who conducted the interview, told him it would be about ten days or so until he heard back regarding whether he would be moving forward to a second interview with Mike, the Senior Vice President.

Like every day, Jeff started with a 6:00 a.m. alarm, by 6:45 Jeff had his coffee brewing and had taken his dog for a morning walk. By 7:00, Jeff was reading the highlights of the day's news and checking up on his emails and social media—making sure he was in the know.

Jeff was a morning person, always ready to tackle the day's obstacles. He would adapt and conquer his daily routine, as well as adjust on the fly and navigate back on course, if need be, to complete the day in a positive, upbeat way.

Jeff paced around his off-campus apartment at PolyTech, a few cars zipped by the closed windows, a few dogs were barking off in the distance, and the brakes of the city local bus could be heard stopping to pick up passengers at the corner.

Jeff knew his window of being called back was shrinking, however Jeff, the hard-nosed young man that he was, knew he gave it his best in the two-hour interview with Frank from HR. This Monday morning, coming out of the weekend Jeff's attitude was on point, and he knew by Wednesday or Thursday he would hear something.

By 8:00 Jeff fed his dog Zeus, ate his normal go to meal of eggs and pre-cooked bacon—got his workout clothes on, and leashed Zeus

DEDICATION

This book is dedicated to all college graduates—give them a reason to hire you.

A Tale of Two College Graduates Who Landed the Interview
Amy and Jeff

Published by: Red Bike Publishing

Published in the United States of America
www.redbikepublishing.com

Library of Congress Control Number: 2022933964

ISBN 13: 13: 978-1-936800-39-1

A Tale of Two College Graduates

Who Landed the Interview

Amy and Jeff

Jim Serger

RED BIKE
PUBLISHING, LLC

A Tale of Two College Graduates

Who Landed the Interview

Amy and Jeff

Jim Serger

To. _____

From. _____

www.ingramcontent.com/pod-product-compliance
Lightning Source LLC
Chambersburg PA
CBHW070700190326
41458CB00046B/6800/J